THE BORDERS' LAST DAYS OF S'

by
W.A.C. Smith

A1 Pacific 4-6-2 No. 60142, 'Edward Fletcher', approaches Reston southbound with a freight train, 24 August, 1963. The name honoured a former North Eastern Railway locomotive superintendent.

Text and photographs © W.A.C. Smith, 2002.
First published in the United Kingdom, 2002,
reprinted 2004, 2008
by Stenlake Publishing Ltd.
Telephone: 01290 551122
www.stenlake.co.uk

ISBN 9781840332247

A3 Pacific 4-6-2 No. 60091, 'Captain Cuttle', passes Reston with the 11.30 a.m. from Peterborough to Edinburgh, 24 August, 1963. The locomotive's unusual name came from the winner of the 1922 Derby. Reston Station was closed in 1964.

INTRODUCTION

Once there were seven rail crossings of the Anglo–Scottish border – with an eighth forming part of a First World War munitions system – but only two now remain, carrying the east and west coast main lines respectively. The first railway crossing was made by the North British Railway in 1846 with its line from Edinburgh through Dunbar and along the coast to Berwick-on-Tweed, the actual crossing being at Lamberton Toll some two and a half miles north of the town. With the spanning of the River Tweed in 1850 by the Royal Border Bridge at Berwick, a direct line of communication was established from Edinburgh with Newcastle by means of the York, Newcastle & Berwick (later North Eastern) Railway which had reached Tweedmouth in 1847. From York the Great Northern Railway carried the route on to London Kings Cross.

The Caledonian Railway was promoted from the English side of the border and the line crossed this by means of the Sark Bridge at Gretna and then went northwards by way of Lockerbie and Annandale, a route decided upon after a Parliamentary tussle with Scottish supporters of a longer, albeit easier, route through Nithsdale. The 'Caley' line was opened from Carlisle to both Edinburgh and Glasgow in 1848, with through trains from Birmingham and London Euston going over what was to later become the London & North Western Railway.

In 1850 the Glasgow & South Western Railway was formed by the amalgamation of the Glasgow, Paisley, Kilmarnock & Ayr and the Glasgow, Dumfries & Carlisle railways and had running powers over the Caledonian Railway from Gretna Junction into Carlisle. From 1876 through trains were run by this route between London St Pancras and Glasgow St Enoch in conjunction with the Midland Railway.

The single track Solway Junction Railway, in which the Caledonian Railway had a strong financial interest, was opened for goods and mineral traffic in 1869 (for passengers in 1870) and, intended for what was mistakenly seen as a lucrative trade in iron ore from West Cumberland to the Lanarkshire iron and steel works, ran from Kirtlebridge (on the Caledonian main line) to Annan, then across the Solway to join the Silloth branch of the North British Railway, before striking southwards to Brayton on the Maryport & Carlisle Railway – the Solway estuary being crossed by means of a mile long viaduct carried on cast iron piers.

During the Railway Mania of 1845 the Caledonian Extension Railway was promoted and planned as a 104 mile trunk route running from Ayr to Berwick by way of Muirkirk, Peebles, Galashiels and Kelso. However, finance was not forthcoming and it was left to the North British Railway to serve the mill towns along the Tweed with the Edinburgh & Hawick Railway which opened in 1849. Taking the name 'Waverley Route' from the novels of Sir Walter Scott, this extended to Carlisle in 1862 by means of the Border Union Railway, running through sparsely populated country to enter England at Kershopefoot and with branches from Riddings Junction to Langholm and from Longtown to Gretna.

Also in 1862 the Border Counties Railway opened, running from isolated Riccarton Junction, south of Hawick, crossing the border at Deadwater and traversing hill country to Hexham on the Newcastle and Carlisle section of the North Eastern Railway; over this latter the North British obtained running powers to Newcastle, but only by granting the English company reciprocal powers between Berwick and Edinburgh. In 1865 the Border Counties were joined at Reedsmouth Junction by the Wansbeck Valley line of the North British from Morpeth on the East Coast main line.

From the Waverley Route the North British gained access to the Cumberland coast by acquisition of the Carlisle & Silloth Bay Railway and Docks Company, while from 1876, when the Midland Railway completed its Settle & Carlisle line, an express service was put on between Edinburgh and London St Pancras.

The North British had also been constructing, and/or purchasing, what became a network of interlinked branches serving the Border towns. The first, in 1850, was from St Boswells to a connection at Kelso with an English branch from Tweedmouth which crossed the border at Carham.

The Jedburgh Railway from Roxburgh Junction was opened in 1856, in which year Selkirk was reached from Galashiels. Ten years later the Peebles Railway, from Eskbank on the Waverley Route and dating from 1855, was extended to Galashiels; from 1864 Peebles was also served by a Caledonian branch from Symington on the West Coast main line. The cross-country Tweedside line was duplicated in 1865 by the Berwickshire Railway from Duns (which had been reached in 1849 from Reston on the East Coast main line), running through Greenlaw to St Boswells and including a nineteen arch viaduct over the Tweed. From Coldstream on the Tweedside line – the station was on the English side of the river although the village was in Scotland – the North Eastern Railway opened in 1887 a thirty-five and a quarter mile line through rural Northumberland by way of Wooler to Alnwick where it joined with a branch from Alnmouth on the main line.

The Eyemouth branch from Burnmouth, five and half miles north of Berwick, was not completed until 1891, and the last of the Border lines, the Lauder Light Railway from Fountainhall on the Waverley Route, was opened in 1901.

Closures started in 1915 with withdrawal of the meagre passenger service between Longtown and Gretna, while the first cross-border closure was that of the Solway Junction line, its lengthy viaduct being condemned in 1921 although not demolished until the mid-1930s.

The Railway Grouping of 1923 saw the North British and North Eastern railways becoming part of the London & North Eastern Railway, with the Caledonian and Glasgow & South Western both going to the London, Midland & Scottish Railway. For the next twenty-five years things went on very much as before, the only closures (to passengers) being the Coldstream to Alnwick line in 1930 and the Lauder branch in 1932.

The monolithic British Railways organisation came into being in 1948 and hopes were high for the future of the network, but closures were soon to commence, the first in the Borders being of Peebles West in 1950, then Duns and Selkirk in 1951, followed by the Morpeth–Reedsmouth section in 1952 and the Borders Counties line in 1956. However, prior to this, nature had taken a hand when, in August 1948, flood damage caused by torrential rain brought about permanent closure of the Berwickshire Railway between Duns and Greenlaw, withdrawal of the Jedburgh branch passenger service and breached the freight line through Wooler. The Eyemouth branch was also closed, by damage to its Eye Water viaduct, and a passenger service was not restored until the following June while washouts along the East Coast main line resulted in expresses such as 'The Flying Scotsman' and 'Queen of Scots Pullman' being diverted via the Waverley Route and Tweedside line.

The run down of the system intensified during the Beeching era, culminating in the devastating closure of the Waverley Route on 6 January, 1969. This closure showed only too well the indifference of government, any government, to the future of the country's railways, closure procedures having been initiated by a Conservative administration and implemented by a Labour administration.

Today politicians promise a railway renaissance and there is even talk of restoring a service between Edinburgh and Galashiels, but the current Railtrack fiasco, along with a lack of any meaningful financing for what remains of our railway network, does little to inspire confidence in the future.

Having traversed the truncated Berwickshire Railway from the main line at Reston, B1 4-6-0 No. 61324 draws out of Duns with the 'Scottish Rambler No. 2' railtour of 14 April, 1963.

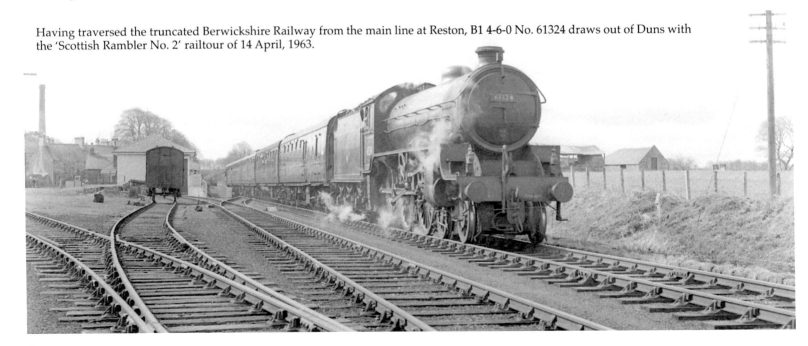

V2 2-6-2 No. 60806 runs into Burnmouth Station with the 3.50 p.m. from Edinburgh to Berwick, 18 July, 1959. The connecting train for Eyemouth waits in the bay platform.

The Berwickshire fishing port of Eyemouth was served by a three mile branch from Burnmouth on the East Coast main line. On 18 July, 1959, the local Gala Day, J39 0-6-0 No. 64843 was working the service and was photographed with the 4.00 p.m. departure. The harbour, crowded with fishing boats, is in the background.

Also on 18 July, 1959, I photographed the Eyemouth branch train bound for the main line at Burnmouth and passing Biglawburn siding, half a mile out of the terminus and serving a roadside oil storage tank.

Another view of Eyemouth Station on 18 July, 1959, with No. 64843 now heading the 5.10 p.m. to Burnmouth.

On a wintry 4 January, 1965, V2 2-6-2 No. 60846 pulls out of Marshall Meadows Yard, one mile north of Berwick, with an Edinburgh bound freight train.

No. 60011, 'Empire of India', one of the LNER's famous A4 4-6-2 streamlined Pacifics (known as 'Streaks' to trainspotters of the day) comes to a stand in Berwick Station with the 11.00 a.m. express from Kings Cross to Glasgow Queen Street, 18 July, 1959. Sister engine 'Mallard' holds the world speed record for steam traction, having reached 126 mph in 1938. It can now be seen at the National Railway Museum in York.

A3 Pacific 4-6-2 No. 60080, 'Dick Turpin', comes off the Royal Border Bridge at Berwick with the 4.18 p.m. from Newcastle, 30 August, 1954.

A2 Pacific 4-6-2 No. 60538, 'Velocity', crosses the Royal Border Bridge at Berwick with the 10.10 a.m. from Kings Cross to Glasgow, 19 August, 1961. The bridge was completed in 1850 and has twenty-eight arches at a maximum height of 120 feet above the River Tweed, although today its appearance is somewhat marred by electrification masts. The locomotive was built at Doncaster Works in 1948 and, appropriately enough, carried the name of the racehorse which had won the Doncaster Cup in 1906 and 1907.

Class D30 4-4-0 No. 62424, 'Claverhouse', is serviced at Tweedmouth depot on 12 June, 1954, after working into Berwick from the Tweedside line. This class of former North British Railway passenger locomotives, which dated from the time of the First World War, bore the names of characters from the novels of Sir Walter Scott and in their early days were used for express passenger trains over the Waverley Route. No. 62424 was scrapped in 1957 and Tweedmouth depot was closed in 1966.

Class K3 2-6-0 No. 61969 in Tweedmouth shed yard, 12 June, 1954. These express goods locomotives were of a Great Northern Railway design dating from 1920 and, adopted by the LNER as a standard design while incorporating various improvements over the years, were built until 1937. Tweedmouth had an allocation of them for use on freight trains to Tyneside and Edinburgh, while others, based at Edinburgh St Margaret's and Carlisle Canal, worked regularly over the Waverley Route with the crews changing over at Hawick. The last of the class was withdrawn in 1962.

On 12 June, 1954, the roundhouse at Tweedmouth motive power depot contained J25 0-6-0 No. 65727 and J39s Nos. 64941 and 64868. The J25 had been built by the North Eastern Railway at Gateshead in 1902 while the J39s were an LNER design dating from 1926. Construction of these continued at Darlington Works until 1941.

Photographed at Coldstream, on the Tweedside line, on 14 April, 1963, B1 4-6-0 No. 61324 resumes haulage of the 'Scottish Rambler No.2' railtour after the train had made a side trip to Wooler hauled by ex-LMS class 2MT 2-6-0 No. 46474. The B1 then continued to Hawick where A3 Pacific 4-6-2 No. 60041, 'Salmon Trout', took over for the remainder of the journey from Edinburgh to Carlisle.

Coldstream Station on 25 September, 1961, with standard class 2MT 2-6-0 No. 78046 heading the 4.00 p.m. train from St Boswells to Berwick and conveying five passengers. From 1955 the through service over the Tweedside line had been reduced from four trains each way daily to two and several intermediate stations were closed.

Another view of No. 78046 with the 4.00 p.m. train from St Boswells to Berwick on 25 September, 1961. This photograph was taken at Kelso where the locomotive was about to reverse into the siding at the station to pick up a pair of vans loaded with parcels traffic. Twenty-six minutes were allowed for the manoeuvre.

Seven years previously, and veteran G5 ex-North Eastern Railway 0-4-4T No. 67268 takes water at Kelso while in charge of the 3.28 p.m. Berwick to St Boswells train, 12 June, 1954. No. 67268 was withdrawn in 1955 after almost sixty years of service.

B1 4-6-0 No. 61324 leaving Jedburgh, a Border town bereft of passenger trains since 1949. Photographed on 14 April, 1963, it was heading for Roxburgh Junction with the 'Scottish Rambler No. 2' railtour which then joined the Waverley Route at St Boswells.

The steeply graded and sharply curved Waverley Route ran for ninety-eight and a quarter miles from Edinburgh to Carlisle and had summits at Falahill (880 feet above sea level), reached by a fifteen mile climb, much of it at 1 in 70, and, following this, at Whitrope (1,006 feet), eleven miles south of Hawick. On 11 May, 1963, B1 4-6-0 No. 61351 was photographed topping Falahill with the 12.05 p.m. semi-fast train from Hawick to Edinburgh.

On a sunny 18 April, 1965, A4 Pacific 4-6-2 No. 60031, 'Golden Plover', stands at Galashiels with the 'Scottish Rambler No. 4' railtour en route from Glasgow Queen Street to Carlisle, by way of Edinburgh and the Waverley Route. With ongoing dieselisation, this locomotive survived for only another six months.

On 25 September, 1961, I was surprised to find Western Region class 7 Britannia Pacific 4-6-2 No. 70018, 'Flying Dutchman', at the head of the 1.28 p.m. train from Carlisle to Edinburgh Waverley. It transpired, however, that locomotives of this class in Wales had been transferred a fortnight previously to the London Midland Region, with two going to Carlisle Canal motive power depot and six to Kingmoor motive power depot. I photographed No. 70018 leaving Melrose at a spot which is today occupied by a road going through the station site.

A3 Pacific 4-6-2 No. 60093, 'Coronach', arrives at Melrose with the 2.36 p.m. train from Edinburgh to Carlisle, 25 September, 1961. This locomotive, built in 1928 and scrapped in 1962, was a familiar sight on the Waverley Route as it was shedded at Carlisle Canal for many years. The name came from a Derby and St Leger winner.

On 4 April, 1959, the Branch Line Society ran a memorable 'Scott Country' railtour, powered by D34 4-4-0 No. 62471, 'Glen Falloch'. Photographed at St Boswells, the train started from Galashiels, taking in the Selkirk and Jedburgh branches and part of the former Berwickshire Railway.

The 'Scott Country' railtour of 4 April, 1959, photographed at Gordon Station en route from St Boswells to Greenlaw.

In brilliant spring sunshine the 'Scott Country' tour reached the end of the line at rural Greenlaw, 4 April, 1959.

The weather was very different when Standard class 4MT 2-6-0 No. 76050 arrived at St Boswells with the 9.59 a.m. from Berwick on the last day of the Tweedside service, 13 June, 1964.

C16 ex-North British Railway 4-4-2T, no. 67489, waits in the bay platform at St Boswells with the 4.05 p.m. train to Kelso and Berwick, 3 September, 1955.

A fine summer evening and a scene which had remained almost unchanged for half a century as G5 0-4-4T No. 67268 awaits departure from St Boswells with the 7.15 p.m. to Berwick via Kelso and Tweedmouth, 12 June, 1954. J36 0-6-0 No. 65331 and a J35 0-6-0 stand outside the small locomotive shed.

A3 Pacific 4-6-2 No. 60093, 'Coronach', leaves St Boswells with the 2.36 p.m. from Edinburgh to Carlisle, 25 September, 1961.

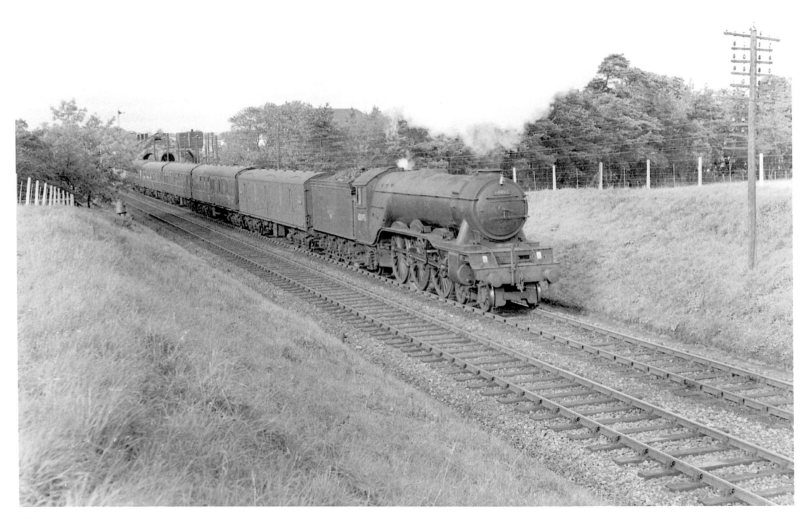

At Hawick Station the platforms extended onto the curving Teviot viaduct some 40 feet above the river. On 3 September, 1955, class 4MT 2-6-0 No. 76046 was awaiting departure with the 4.32 p.m. train over the Border Counties line to Hexham and then to Newcastle.

The main locomotive depot on the Waverley Route was at Hawick (its British Railway code was 64G, the number affixed to its locomotives' smokeboxes) with smaller sheds at Riccarton, St Boswells and Galashiels. Regular duties for Hawick locomotives and men included local workings to Edinburgh and Carlisle, workings on the Border Counties line, and banking of

heavy trains to Whitrope summit. Power for through trains was provided by locomotives from either Carlisle Canal and Edinburgh St Margarets. At its peak Hawick shed employed 150 staff and had an allocation of twenty or more locomotives. However, increasing dieselisation caused the depot's closure in January, 1966. On 3 September, 1955, class J36 0-6-0 No. 65331 and D30 4-4-0 No. 62435, 'Norna' (left), were photographed in the shed yard, while five years later J35 0-6-0 No. 64494 and C16 4-4-2T No. 67489 were also caught by the camera.

No. 60532, 'Blue Peter', takes water at Hawick on 8 October, 1966, with a British Railways special excursion from Edinburgh to Carlisle (outward via Hawick and returning via Carstairs at a fare of thirty-five shillings). This engine was described as 'the last remaining A2 Pacific locomotive'. The 270 passengers were to enjoy a day out, which included a visit to Kingmoor motive power depot, in fine weather and with 'Blue Peter' attaining 80 mph on the return journey. This very enjoyable tour was organised by Ron Cotton, a British Railways manager who went on to save the scenic Settle & Carlisle line from closure. Just a pity that he was not in a position to do the same for the Waverley Route. However, the locomotive, which bears the name of the 1931 Derby winner, has been preserved and, when not on main line outings, can be seen on the North Yorkshire Moors Railway.

Despite withdrawal of the passenger service over the Border Counties line in 1956 a freight service was maintained to Reedsmouth and Bellingham by means of the Wansbeck Valley line from Morpeth. This ended in 1963 and on 11 October, a few weeks before closure, I joined the twice weekly train for a farewell trip and photographed J27 ex-North Eastern Railway 0-6-0 No. 65819 (from Blaydon depot) doing some shunting at the end of the line at Bellingham.

Steam to the rescue! On 13 June, 1964, Peak class diesel No. D27 failed north of Newcastleton with the up 'Waverley' express (the 10.15 a.m. Edinburgh Waverley to London St Pancras service). The train was taken over by A3 Pacific 4-6-2 No. 60077, 'The White Knight' (a character from *Alice in Wonderland* and the name carried by the winner of the 1907 and 1908 Ascot Gold Cup), commandeered from a northbound freight train. The diesel locomotive was dumped at Newcastleton and the Pacific then ran the train tender first to Carlisle.

B1 4-6-0 No. 61242, 'Alexander Reith Gray', sweeps down Liddesdale towards Riddings Junction with a southbound Waverley Route freight train from Edinburgh to Carlisle, 6 April, 1963. The locomotive carried the name of an LNER director.

Langholm, bypassed by the Waverley Route, was served by a seven mile branch from Riddings Junction where Ivatt ex-LMS class 4MT 2-6-0 No. 43000 was photographed arriving with the 6.32 p.m. from the border town to Carlisle on 6 April, 1963.

There were two intermediate stations on the Langholm branch and on 6 April, 1963, 4MT 2-6-0 No. 43011 was photographed soon after leaving Gilknockie with the 3.30 p.m. from Langholm to Carlisle.

The terminus at Langholm is seen here on 1 September, 1954, with J39 0-6-0 No. 64884 heading the 3.28 p.m. departure to Carlisle. The passenger service ended in 1964 and today a small cairn in a housing estate marks the site of the station.

B1 4-6-0 No. 61099 stands at Longtown, a village once thronged with munitions workers, with a freight train from Millerhill Yard at Edinburgh to Carlisle's Kingmoor New Yard, 6 April, 1963. The diesel hauled 1.40 p.m. passenger train from Carlisle to Edinburgh has brought a relief crew for the freight train.

The North British Railway successfully developed Silloth as a port and holiday resort on the Solway, but early British Railway days saw a sharp decline in freight traffic. In an attempt to retain passengers diesel multiple units were introduced as early as 1954, but steam trains were still required during holiday periods for their greater carrying capacity and at Silloth on Easter Monday, 11 April, 1955, I photographed J39 0-6-0 No. 64875 with the 4.48 p.m. departure for Carlisle. The Beeching axe fell in 1964 and on the last night protesters staged a sit-down on the tracks, a scene to be repeated less than five years later at Newcastleton on the Waverley Route.

British Railways class 7 Britannia Pacific 4-6-2 No. 70041, 'Sir John Moore', gathers speed past Port Carlisle Junction with the 9.25 a.m. train from Crewe to Perth, 8 May, 1965. The Waverley Route can be seen veering off to the right.

With the castle and cathedral of the 'Border City' in the background, Coronation class 4-6-2 No. 46251, 'City of Nottingham', crosses the River Eden at Etterby with a Stephenson Locomotive Society special train from Birmingham, 12 July, 1964. Less than three months later all of these magnificent locomotives had gone for scrap, although happily three survive in preservation. The bridge on the right was built as a wartime measure in 1942.

The large Kingmoor locomotive depot was built by the Caledonian Railway on open ground at Etterby, north of the city, and originated as a timber structure in 1877, being rebuilt in brick during the First World War. On 8 October, 1966, class 4MT 2-6-0 No. 43049 was photographed while taking water at the north end of the shed yard. The LMS built coaling tower is in the background. Despite being less than two years from the end of British Railways steam forty locomotives were active at Kingmoor that afternoon, with a similar number out of use. The depot closed to steam on 31 December, 1967.

On a bright afternoon in 1965 V2 2-6-2 No. 60816 and A3 Pacific 4-6-2 No. 60100, 'Spearmint', enjoy a well earned rest at Kingmoor motive power depot after working freight trains over the Waverley Route. Prior to its closure in 1963, they would have used Canal shed.

Class 4MT 2-6-0 (a 'Mogul' in railway parlance) No. 43045 passes under Victoria viaduct and arrives at platform four of Carlisle Citadel Station with the 10.48 a.m. from Langholm, 6 April, 1963.

Compound 4-4-0 No. 40913 about to leave platform one of Carlisle Citadel with the 5.51 p.m. local for Dumfries and Glasgow St Enoch, 1 September, 1954. Beside it, Jubilee 4-6-0 No. 45704, 'Leviathan', waits to follow with a parcels train.

Six years on and the station's overall roof has been cut back and new platform awnings have been erected. Coronation Pacific 4-6-2 No. 46230, 'Duchess of Buccleuch', heads the 7.35 p.m. to Glasgow St Enoch via Dumfries on a very wet 23 May, 1960, while Jubilee 4-6-0 No. 45642, 'Boscawen', is about to depart with the afternoon train from Liverpool and Manchester to Glasgow Central via Beattock.

Built by the LNER in 1924, but by now sporting a double chimney and German style smoke deflectors, A3 Pacific 4-6-2 No. 60052, 'Prince Palatine' (the racehorse of this name was winner of the 1911 St Leger), stands at platform four of Carlisle Citadel on 5 June, 1965, with a Scottish Locomotive Preservation Fund special train, returning to Edinburgh via the Waverley Route. Outward the route had been by way of Berwick and Hexham. The fund was to be successful in purchasing a former Caledonian Railway 0-6-0 locomotive which can now be seen on the Strathspey Railway at Aviemore.

In the penultimate year of British Railways steam Black Five 4-6-0 No. 44672 starts away from platform three of Carlisle Citadel with a relief train from Leeds to Glasgow, 5 August, 1967.